3/10

Dr. Seuss

Laura Hamilton Waxman

⌐ LERNER PUBLICATIONS COMPANY • MINNEAPOLIS

For Shaan, Caleb, and Yana, two generations of Dr. Seuss lovers

Illustrations by Tad Butler

Copyright © 2010 by Laura Hamilton Waxman
Illustrations © 2010 by Lerner Publishing Group, Inc.

Lerner Publications Company
A division of Lerner Publishing Group, Inc.
241 First Avenue North
Minneapolis, MN 55401 U.S.A.

Website address: www.lernerbooks.com

Library of Congress Cataloging-in-Publication Data

Waxman, Laura Hamilton.
    Dr. Seuss / by Laura Hamilton Waxman.
      p.   cm. — (History maker biographies)
    Includes bibliographical references and index.
    ISBN 978–0–7613–5206–8 (lib. bdg. : alk. paper)
    1. Seuss, Dr.—Juvenile literature. 2. Authors, American—20th century—
Biography—Juvenile literature. 3. Illustrators—United States—Biography—
Juvenile literature. 4. Children's literature—Authorship—Juvenile literature.
I. Title.
PS3513.E2Z928 2010
813'.52—dc22 [B]   2009018358

Manufactured in the United States of America
1 – VI – 12/15/2009

TABLE OF CONTENTS

INTRODUCTION

Most people have heard of Dr. Seuss. Not as many people know that his real name was Ted Geisel. Ted began writing children's books in the 1930s. His books were different from many children's books at the time. They didn't teach children how to follow rules. Ted's books encouraged readers to use their imaginations. His playful stories made reading fun.

Ted's books were full of made-up people, animals, and places. He even used a made-up name for himself. As Dr. Seuss, Ted wrote about Horton, the Grinch, and the Cat in the Hat. He wrote about a fox in socks and about green eggs and ham. Ted's big imagination filled the pages of his Dr. Seuss books. They are some of the most popular books ever written for children.

This is his story.

1 YOUNG ARTIST

Theodor Seuss Geisel was born in Springfield, Massachusetts, on March 2, 1904. His parents were Henrietta Seuss Geisel and Theodor Robert Geisel. They called their little boy Ted.

Ted had an older sister named Margaretha, or Marnie. They each had their own bedroom in the family's house on Fairfield Street. Ted's room was on the second floor. From there, he could hear animal sounds coming from the nearby Springfield Zoo.

Ted was filled with curiosity and fun. He liked to dress up in costumes from the attic. He liked to watch bicycles, wagons, and horse-drawn carriages going down nearby Mulberry Street. He liked to play and laugh with his friends.

This picture shows Springfield about 1910, when Ted was a young boy.

A crowd watches the alligators at the Springfield Zoo.

Most of all, Ted loved to draw. He almost always had a pencil in his hand. The zoo was one of his favorite places to practice drawing. He drew pictures of all the animals he saw there. But his drawings never came out quite right. The animals always looked a little strange.

Even so, Ted's parents were proud of his creativity. They encouraged him to keep using his imagination. Theodor Geisel also taught his son about hard work. Mr. Geisel helped run his family's brewery. The company made and sold beer.

Ted's mother gave him a love of stories and words. She sang rhymes to him and his sister before bed. She also brought home children's books for them to read.

At the time, many books taught children lessons. They told children how to follow rules and behave. Ted didn't care about the lessons. He just loved the books for their rhymes and drawings. Some of his favorite books used funny made-up words. Other books told of imaginary creatures such as the Snook, the Rigglerok, and the Tootle Bird. These books helped set Ted's imagination free.

Ted's family lived in this house in Springfield. Ted's mother made reading at home a fun pastime.

Ted also read comic strips in the newspaper. One of his favorite comics was called *Krazy Kat*. This black cat walked on two legs, talked, and wore a bowtie.

Ted liked reading for fun. But he didn't enjoy reading schoolbooks or studying. He would rather go to the movies or joke with friends. He wasn't loud or outspoken. He just knew how to have fun. He was always making people laugh.

TED AND WORLD WAR I

In 1914, when Ted was ten, World War I broke out in Europe. The United States joined the war in 1917. U.S. soldiers helped fight against Germany. Americans started thinking of Germans as their enemies. Ted's grandfather had come from Germany. Ted had always been proud of his family's German past. But some people in Springfield called him and his family hurtful names. He never forgot how that felt. As an adult, he always tried to treat others fairly.

The only thing Ted seemed serious about was drawing. He stayed serious about it even in high school. There he decided to sign up for an art class. But the class didn't go well. The teacher wanted Ted to follow her rules. Ted didn't like being told how to draw. He quit the class that first day.

Ted went to Central High School in Springfield.

Ted began to draw funny cartoons for his school newspaper. It was called the *Central Recorder*. Ted's cartoons used art and words to make jokes. His cartoons showed off his playful imagination. They made people laugh. So did his poems and stories. He had a way of bringing out the silly side of life.

Ted graduated from high school in 1921. He was seventeen years old. He had grown into a tall, handsome young man. But in some ways, he hadn't grown up at all. He still liked having fun. And he still loved using his imagination.

AT THE ZOO

In 1919, the United States outlawed alcohol. It was against the law to buy or sell it. The Geisel family brewery went out of business. Ted's father had to get a new job. He ended up running Springfield's public parks. This large area included the Springfield Zoo. Ted loved going on private tours of the zoo with his dad.

2 CLEVER CARTOONIST

Ted went to Dartmouth College in the fall of 1921. His new school was four hours away in New Hampshire. Ted still didn't care much about his schoolwork. He disliked studying as much as ever. He just wanted to draw and have fun.

Right away, Ted started working for the college's magazine. It was called the *Jack-o-Lantern*. Students called it *Jacko* for short. Clever stories and funny cartoons filled the magazine's pages. Many of the comics were drawn by Ted.

Ted kept coming up with new ideas for *Jacko*. For fun, he signed some of his cartoons with made-up names. One name was LeSieg—Geisel spelled backward. He also used his middle name, Seuss.

Many of Ted's cartoons showed funny people doing funny things. Other cartoons were about imaginary animals. Ted drew an animal with an umbrella for a tail. He drew a catbird and a dogfish. He drew a skinny snake riding a skateboard. His imagination seemed to grow and grow.

Ted spent many hours drawing and writing. But he always made time for fun. People invited him to parties and dinners. They liked having such a charming and friendly guy around.

Ted drew this cartoon for an article in Jacko.

In 1924, Ted became *Jacko*'s editor in chief. That put him in charge of the whole magazine. He loved the job. But it didn't last. He graduated from Dartmouth in the summer of 1925. It was time to choose a grown-up career.

Most of Ted's college friends planned on becoming lawyers, bankers, or businessmen. None of those jobs sounded interesting to Ted. Instead, he decided to go overseas to Britain. He became a student there at Oxford University. Perhaps he could study to become a professor.

This building is on the campus of Oxford University.

As usual, Ted made good friends at his new school. One of them was a woman named Helen Palmer. Helen was quiet and kind. She and Ted liked each other right away. They quickly fell in love.

Ted still didn't like schoolwork much. He often got bored listening to his teachers. Instead, he drew silly pictures in his notebooks. One day, Helen saw one of his drawings. "That's a very fine flying cow!" she said. She asked him why he was studying to be a professor. He should try to draw for a living, she told him.

Ted agreed. He quit school that summer. By then, he and Helen were engaged to be married. But they couldn't marry yet. Ted needed to get a job. He had to earn enough money to take care of them.

Ted spent about eight months living in Paris and other European cities. He worked on becoming a better artist. Then he moved back home.

Paris was a popular city for artists.

Many big magazines had offices in New York City.

Ted had decided on a career. He wanted to draw cartoons for a living. Many magazines printed clever cartoons for adults. The biggest magazines were in New York City. Ted hoped one of them would give him work. He sent them samples of his drawings. But no one wanted to hire him.

Helen was working as a teacher in New Jersey. She cheered on Ted in her letters. Her encouragement helped keep him going.

Ted finally got some good news in the summer of 1927. A magazine called the *Saturday Evening Post* agreed to print one of his cartoons. Ted was thrilled. He knew that people around the country read this popular magazine. Even better, the *Post* paid him $25 for his cartoon. It came out in July. He signed it with the name Seuss.

Ted's success gave him courage. He decided to move to New York City. He was determined to get a job as a cartoonist.

3 CHILDREN'S BOOK WRITER

In New York, a popular magazine agreed to hire Ted. The magazine was called *Judge*. Ted did not earn a lot of money as a cartoonist. But he made enough to take care of Helen. He happily married her on October 22, 1927.

Judge magazine had news articles and funny cartoons.

Ted's imagination was as big as ever. He drew many funny cartoons for *Judge*. He signed most of them with a silly name— Dr. Seuss. People loved Dr. Seuss and his clever drawings.

Soon Ted was getting even more work. An advertising agency hired him in 1928. Businesses paid these companies to create ads for them. Ted started drawing ads for a bug spray called Flit. He finished a new ad every three weeks. He always signed them with the name Dr. Seuss.

Ted's clever Flit ads showed up in magazines and thousands of newspapers. The ads made the name Dr. Seuss famous. They also made Ted a lot of money. He and Helen moved to a large apartment in the city. They began taking long summer trips around the world.

Ted used his phrase "Quick, Henry, the Flit!" on many of his Flit ads.

Ted drew art for Standard Oil Co. This is a picture of a Standard Oil gas station in the early 1900s.

Ted worked very hard the rest of the year. He was drawing for several magazines and companies. His artwork helped sell fans, lightbulbs, shaving cream, pens, gasoline, and radios. He even drew art for two children's books. With all this work, he never seemed to run out of ideas. His big imagination kept on going.

Ted liked drawing pictures for children's books. And the books had sold well. He decided to write and draw a children's book of his own. He spent many hours making art for an alphabet story. But no one wanted to print it. Publishing companies didn't think anyone would buy it.

In 1936, Ted and Helen took a trip to Europe. People did not travel by airplane in those days. So Ted and Helen sailed across the Atlantic Ocean on a ship. Ted noticed that the ship's engines clanged to a regular beat. To him the beat sounded like *da da DA, da da DA, da da DA, da da DA*. He started putting words to the beat. Soon he had the beginning of a rhyming children's story. It was about a boy with a wild imagination.

This postcard shows the ship Ted and Helen took across the Atlantic Ocean in 1936.

Back home, Ted worked hard on his story. He remembered how his favorite picture books had opened up his imagination. He wanted his book to do the same thing for readers. He drew lively pictures. He spent hours finding just the right words. And he made sure his story was a lot of fun.

THE GREAT DEPRESSION

Ted earned a good living in the 1930s. Many other Americans were not so lucky. In 1929, the country had begun to have big money problems. Banks shut down. Many Americans lost their savings. Without money they couldn't afford to buy the things they needed. Many stores went out of business. A lot of people lost their jobs. This time became known as the Great Depression. It lasted for more than ten years.

It took Ted six months to get his book just right. He sent it to many publishing companies. But none of them wanted it. It didn't teach children any rules or lessons, they said. They told him it was full of too many crazy, made-up ideas.

Ted felt hopeless. He wanted to burn his story in the fireplace. Then one day, he ran into an old college friend. This friend had just become a children's book editor. He looked at Ted's story and loved it. He agreed to publish it.

The book came out in September 1937. It was called *And to Think That I Saw It on Mulberry Street.* Ted published it under the name Dr. Seuss.

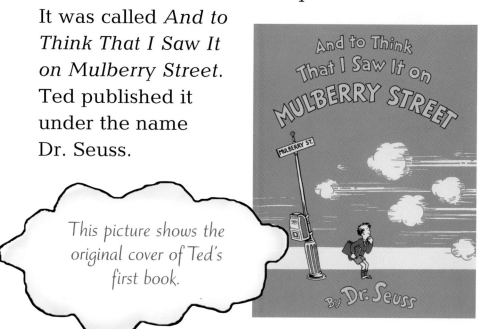

This picture shows the original cover of Ted's first book.

Ted's first book did not sell a lot of copies. Other children's authors were much more popular. Even so, he enjoyed the work. In the next three years, he wrote more books for children. One of them was about a loyal elephant named Horton. It was called *Horton Hatches the Egg*. Readers loved the story of the lovable elephant and his baby elephant-bird. They wanted to read more books by the imaginative Dr. Seuss.

Horton the elephant was popular. People even sold Horton stuffed animals.

4 MILITARY MAN

Life was going well for Ted. But he worried about the rest of the world. World War II had begun in 1939. France and Great Britain were fighting against Germany. Other countries had also joined the fighting. But the United States didn't join. Most Americans did not want anything to do with a war in Europe.

Ted disagreed. He knew that the Germans were mistreating many groups of people. The biggest group was the Jews. Germany's leader had even begun to kill millions of Jewish Europeans. This news upset Ted terribly.

Ted had always used his talents to make people laugh. But he wanted to do something serious. So he started publishing serious cartoons. Many of them were about the war. He wanted to show Americans that the United States needed to join the fight.

Some of Ted's serious cartoons were about Adolf Hitler. In this cartoon, someone reads a book called ADOLF THE WOLF.

The United States finally entered the war in 1941. After that, Ted drew cartoons in support of the war. He also drew cartoons to support the Jews in Europe.

Ted was glad his work helped make a difference. But he didn't think he was doing enough. In 1943, he joined the U.S. military. Ted was almost forty years old. He was too old to be a foot soldier. He could help in other ways.

Ted poses in his military uniform.

The military sent Ted to Hollywood, California. They wanted him to make films for U.S. soldiers. Ted worked on films that helped teach soldiers how to win the war.

World War II ended in 1945. Ted's work with the military was done. He left to make other movies. But he missed writing for kids. He decided to write some more books.

FIGHTING FOR FAIRNESS

Ted's serious cartoons were not only about the war. He drew cartoons about other problems too. One of those problems was racism. This unfair treatment harmed African Americans. Many white people believed African Americans did not deserve to be treated fairly. Ted disagreed. He drew cartoons against racism.

Ted stands with Helen outside their new home in La Jolla, California.

He and Helen also decided to stay in California. They built a new home in the town of La Jolla. The house was as imaginative as Ted's stories. Out of it rose a tower two stories high. From the top, the Geisels could see the whole city.

Ted worked in one room in his new home. He spent many hours there each day. His imagination was bursting with new ideas for books. But turning ideas into good stories was hard. He wanted each of his books to be just right.

Ted wrote books about crazy zoos and wild circuses. He wrote about a big-hearted moose named Thidwick. He wrote a second book about Horton the elephant. It was called *Horton Hears a Who!* The book came out in 1954. Ted's Dr. Seuss books thrilled his readers. Children loved his characters and their wild adventures. Children especially enjoyed the animals Ted invented. The animals had funny names such as the Obsk, the Seersucker, and the Bippo-No-Bungus.

Ted reads Horton Hears a Who! to a four-year-old friend.

Ted works at his typewriter in the 1950s.

One day, a publishing company gave Ted a new idea. The company asked him to write a book for beginning readers. He was given a short list of words to use. They were easy words such as *kite*, *cat*, *fish*, and *hat*. Ted had to write his story using only words from that list. He knew it would be hard. But he wanted to try.

At the time, books for new readers were not very exciting. They didn't tell much of a story. They didn't use much imagination. These books made reading seem boring to many children. Ted wanted to help change that.

He put his imagination to work. He started with a story about a zebra who was a queen. This new idea excited him. Then he realized that *Queen* and *Zebra* were not on his list of words. So he had to start over.

He studied his list again. Soon another story came to him. It was about a walking and talking cat. The cat wore a hat. And he caused lots of trouble.

Ted's book came out in 1957. It was called *The Cat in the Hat*. Children loved it from the start. The story made reading playful and fun. The book sold better than any other book Ted had written.

Ted holds up the cover of his book THE CAT IN THE HAT.

He wrote another popular book that same year. It was called *How the Grinch Stole Christmas.* It's about a grumpy creature who hates everything about the Christmas season.

Ted's latest books earned him many new fans. They made the name Dr. Seuss very famous. At the age of fifty-three, Ted had become a star.

This image shows a scene from the first movie version of How the Grinch Stole Christmas.

5 SUPERSTAR

Of all his books, Ted was most proud of *The Cat in the Hat*. That book began to change how children learned to read. Ted wanted to write more books like it. He was already working on new ideas.

In 1957, he helped set up a new publishing company for young readers. The company published Beginner Books. These books were written for new readers. Ted wrote many Beginner Books. They had funny names such as *Hop on Pop* and *One Fish Two Fish Red Fish Blue Fish*. One of his most popular Beginner Books was called *Green Eggs and Ham*. It came out in 1960.

Ted had become more famous than ever. Millions of children and adults had read his Dr. Seuss books. His fans were curious about the real author. They wanted to know what he was really like.

Ted smiles for reporters in this 1957 photo.

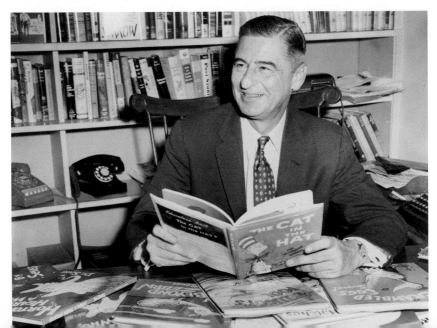

Ted reads THE CAT IN THE HAT to children at a public library.

Ted allowed a few reporters to interview him. He visited schools and bookstores. He even went on TV. But he didn't like talking about himself. He got nervous speaking in front of crowds. He would rather be at home working on a new book.

Helen helped keep Ted's life private. She answered most of his fan letters. She turned away strangers who wanted to see him at home. She took care of him in many ways. But Ted and Helen had begun to drift apart. And Helen's health was failing. She died in 1967.

Ted tried to cheer himself up by writing a new book. He also went on dates with an old friend. Her name was Audrey Dimond.

Audrey was full of energy and curiosity, just like Ted. She made him feel happy again. They married on August 5, 1968. Ted was sixty-four years old.

Ted kept on writing funny books for children. But he also wrote about serious ideas. One of his books was about taking care of the environment. He called it *The Lorax*. Another book was called *The Butter Battle Book*. It spoke against nuclear weapons and nuclear war. This kind of war could kill or harm millions of people.

Audrey watches Ted draw at his desk.

By the age of eighty, Ted had written dozens of books for children. They had changed the way other people wrote for children too. In 1984, he was honored for his important work. He won the famous Pulitzer Prize. Many great writers have won this award. Ted won many other awards too.

Ted was growing older. He wasn't as strong or healthy as he used to be. But he still liked to have fun. He still loved to make people laugh. And he still kept on writing books for children.

IDEA MAN

Reporters and fans often asked Ted, "Where do you get your ideas?" Ted disliked this question. But he knew people expected an answer. Sometimes he made up a story about how he wrote a book. Other times, he gave a silly answer. He liked to say that his ideas came from imaginary places such as Zybliknov and Gletch.

Ted published his last book in 1990. It was called *Oh, the Places You'll Go!* It encouraged readers to have big dreams. It told them to follow those dreams, just as Ted had done.

Ted died the next year. He was eighty-seven years old. By then, 200 million copies of his books had been sold. His imagination and ideas live on. They bring the joy of reading to children each and every day.

Children read THE CAT IN THE HAT at a ceremony in honor of Dr. Seuss. The 2004 ceremony took place in Hollywood, California.

TIMELINE

THEODOR SEUSS GIESEL WAS BORN ON MARCH 2, 1904.

In the year . . .

1921 Ted went to Dartmouth College and worked for the *Jack-O-Lantern.*

1926 he went to Oxford University in Britain and met Helen Palmer. `Age 22`

1927 he returned home to Massachusetts and began drawing cartoons for magazines.

he and Helen married on October 22.

1937 his first book, *And to Think That I Saw It on Mulberry Street,* came out. `Age 33`

1943 he served in the U.S. military during World War II, making films for U.S. soldiers.

1948 he and Helen bought land in La Jolla, California, and built a house there.

1954 his book *Horton Hears a Who!* came out. `Age 50`

1957 he published *The Cat in the Hat* and *How the Grinch Stole Christmas.*

1958 his books *The Cat in the Hat Comes Back* and *Yertle the Turtle* came out.

1960 he published two of his most popular books, *Green Eggs and Ham* and *One Fish Two Fish Red Fish Blue Fish.*

1967 his first wife, Helen, died.

1968 he married Audrey Dimond on August 5. `Age 64`

1971 his book *The Lorax* came out.

1984 he won the Pulitzer Prize. `Age 80`

1990 his last book, *Oh, The Places You'll Go!* was published.

1991 he died on September 24. `Age 87`

2002 the Dr. Seuss National Memorial Sculpture Garden opened.

Dr. Seuss Sculpture Garden

Imagine seeing Dr. Seuss's characters up close. Visitors to the Dr. Seuss National Memorial Sculpture Garden get to do just that. The garden is home to many playful bronze sculptures. All of them are from popular Dr. Seuss books. There are sculptures of Horton, Sam-I-Am, the Grinch, and the Lorax. There's a tower of turtles from *Yertle the Turtle*. One sculpture even shows Ted at his drawing board. Right next to him is the Cat in the Hat. The sculpture garden is located in Ted's hometown of Springfield, Massachusetts.

These bronze sculptures of Ted and the Cat in the Hat are in the National Memorial Sculpture Garden.

FURTHER READING

Belloc, Hilaire. *Cautionary Tales & Bad Child's Book of Beasts.* **Mineolo, NY: Dover Publications, 2008.** Read for yourself some of Ted's favorite childhood books from the early 1900s.

Newell, Peter. *The Hole Book.* **Whitefish, MT: Kessinger Publishing, 2008.** First published in 1908, this was another of young Ted's favorite books.

Seuss, Dr. *Your Favorite Seuss: A Baker's Dozen by the One and Only Dr. Seuss.* **New York: Random House, 2004.** This collection of Dr. Seuss's most-loved stories includes *The Cat in the Hat* and *How the Grinch Stole Christmas*.

Weidt, Maryann N. *Oh, The Places He Went: A Story about Dr. Seuss.* **Minneapolis: Millbrook Press, 1994.** This illustrated biography takes readers on a journey through the life of Dr. Seuss.

WEBSITES

The Dr. Seuss National Memorial Sculpture Garden
http://www.catinthehat.org
This official website includes information about Dr. Seuss, as well as photographs of some sculptures in the garden.

Seussentennial
http://www.kidsreads.com/features/010221-seuss/seuss.asp
This website allows Dr. Seuss fans to test their knowledge with fun online quizzes.

Seussville
http://www.seussville.com
This kid-friendly website was created by the publisher of Dr. Seuss's Beginner Books and includes information and games.

SELECT BIBLIOGRAPHY

Cohen, Charles D. *The Seuss, The Whole Seuss, and Nothing but the Seuss: A Visual Biography of Theodor Seuss Geisel.* New York: Random House, 2004.

Fensch, Thomas. *The Man Who Was Dr. Seuss: The Life and Work of Theodor Geisel.* Woodlands, TX: New Century Books, 2000.

MacDonald, Ruth K. *Dr. Seuss.* Boston: Twayne Publishers, 1988.

Minear, Richard H. *Dr. Seuss Goes to War.* New York: New Press, 1999.

Morgan, Judith, and Neil Morgan. *Dr. Seuss & Mr. Geisel: A Biography.* New York: Random House, 1995.

Nel, Philip. *Dr. Seuss: American Icon.* New York: Continuum International Publishing Group, 2004.

INDEX

Acknowledgments

For photographs and artwork: AP Photo, pp. 4, 19, 34; © Photo Collection Alexander Alland, Sr./CORBIS, p. 7; Connecticut Valley Historical Museum, Springfield, Massachusetts, pp. 8, 9 (Springfield Dept. of Public Works, Building Department), 45; Photography Collection, Miriam and Ira D. Wallach Division of Art, Prints and Photographs, The New York Public Library, Astor, Lenox and Tilden Foundations, p. 11; © Yogi, Inc./CORBIS, p. 14; Dartmouth College Library, *Jack-O-Lantern*, November 26, 1923, p. 15; © William Vandivert/Time & Life Pictures/Getty Images, pp. 16, 17; © Harlingue/Roger Viollet/Getty Images, p. 18; © Buyenlarge/Hulton Archive/Getty Images, p. 22; Mandeville Special Collections, University of California, San Diego, pp. 23, 31; © Hulton Archive/ Getty Images, p. 24; © K.J. Historical/CORBIS, p. 25; "Book Cover", from AND TO THINK THAT I SAW IT ON MULBERRY STREET by Dr. Seuss, copyright TM & copyright © by Dr. Seuss Enterprises, L.P. 1937, renewed 1964. Used by permission of Random House Children's Books, a division of Random House, Inc., p. 27; © Syracuse Newspapers/David Lassman/The Image Works, p. 28; AP Photo/ The New Press, p. 30; © Gene Lester/Hulton Archive/Getty Images, pp. 33, 36, 40; © John Bryson/Time & Life Pictures/Getty Images, p. 35; © MGM/Courtesy Everett Collection, p. 37; Library of Congress (LC-USZ62-116956), p. 39; © James L. Amos/CORBIS, p. 41; © Vince Bucci/Getty Images, p. 43. Front cover: © John Bryson/Time & Life Pictures/Getty Images. Back cover: © D. Hurst/Alamy.
For quoted material: p. 17, Judith and Neil Morgan, *Dr. Seuss & Mr. Geisel: A Biography* (New York: Random House, 1995).